UNDERSTANDING
WORLD RELIGIONS

Understanding
Islam

Don Nardo

ReferencePoint
Press®

San Diego, CA

© 2019 ReferencePoint Press, Inc.
Printed in the United States

For more information, contact:
ReferencePoint Press, Inc.
PO Box 27779
San Diego, CA 92198
www. ReferencePointPress.com

LIBRARY OF CONGRESS CATALOGING-IN-PUBLICATION DATA

Name: Nardo, Don, 1947– author.
Title: Understanding Islam/By Don Nardo.
Description: San Diego, CA: ReferencePoint Press, 2019. | Series:
    Understanding World Religions | Includes bibliographical references and
    index.
Identifiers: LCCN 2018005889 (print) | LCCN 2018007922 (ebook) | ISBN
    9781682824665 (eBook) | ISBN 9781682824658 (hardback)
Subjects: LCSH: Islam.
Classification: LCC BP161.3 (ebook) | LCC BP161.3 .N36 2019 (print) | DDC
    297—dc23
LC record available at https://lccn.loc.gov/2018005889

CONTENTS

World Religions: By the Numbers

According to a 2017 Pew Research Center demographic analysis, Christians were the largest religious group in the world in 2015. However, that may be changing. The same analysis projects Muslims to be the world's fastest-growing major religious group over the next four decades.

Percent of World Population

- 6.9%
- 5.7%
- 0.8%
- 0.2%
- 15.1%
- 16%
- 31.2%
- 24.1%

Legend:
- Christians
- Muslims
- Hindus
- Buddhists
- Folk religions
- Jews
- Other religions
- Unaffiliated

Number of People in 2015 (in billions)

- Christians — 2.3
- Muslims — 1.8
- Unaffiliated — 1.2
- Hindus — 1.1
- Buddhists — 0.5
- Folk religions — 0.4
- Other religions — 0.1
- Jews — 0.01

Estimated Percent Change in Population Size, 2015–2060

- Muslims — +70
- Christians — +34
- Hindus — +27
- Jews — +15
- Folk religions — +5
- Unaffiliated — +3
- Other religions — 0
- Buddhists — -7

32% growth in overall global population

Source: Conrad Hackett and David McClendon, "Christians Remain World's Largest Religious Group, but They Are Declining in Europe," Pew Research Center: The Changing Global Religious Landscape, April 5, 2017. www.pewresearch.org.

The Remarkable Unity of Islam

Islam is one of the three main monotheistic faiths, along with Christianity and Judaism. Followers of Islam, called Muslims, worship the same God as Christians and Jews and recognize as holy prophets Judeo-Christian figures such as Moses and Jesus. The primary difference between Islam and these two other faiths is that Muslims recognize a later, and final, prophet—Muhammad. Born in early medieval times, he claimed to receive new revelations from God and started a new faith based on them.

Today, more than fourteen centuries later, Muslims number nearly 2 billion around the globe, accounting for more than 20 percent of the world's population. That makes Islam the second-biggest faith after Christianity. Islam is also a constantly expanding religion. Census records show that Muslims make up the fastest-growing religious minority in both Europe and the United States. In addition, Islam is the youngest of the world's major faiths, having emerged in the seventh century in the Arabian Peninsula.

Most Muslims, like members of the other major religions, desire that all peoples live together in peace. One of the more popular modern prayers said by Muslims in many lands says in part: "In the name of God, the compassionate, the merciful, look with compassion on the whole human family; take away the controversial teachings of arrogance, divisions, and hatreds which have badly infected our hearts; break down the walls that separate us; reunite us in bonds of love [and] harmony."[1]

Those Who Left

The divisions and hatreds mentioned in the prayer are a reference to differences, in some cases deep-seated ones, among various Muslim groups. In particular, most Muslims condemn violent Islamist

5

Muslim women offer prayers in a mosque in Lahore, Pakistan. One of the most popular prayers among modern Muslims asks God to help all humankind live in harmony.

organizations like al Qaeda and the Islamic State of Iraq and Syria (ISIS), which spread hatred and employ terror tactics. A number of modern scholars have compared the members of ISIS with the Kharijites (KAR-ee-ites), the very first Muslim group to break away from mainstream Islam, not long after the faith's founding.

The story of the Kharijites illustrates several key aspects of Islam, including the high level of devotion to the faith among all of its members, no matter what their differences might be. The Kharijites' temporary rise to prominence occurred in the years immediately following the death of the Prophet Muhammad in 632. After he passed, a series of his family members assumed control of the Muslim community, or *ummah*, in Arabia. One of them, his son-in-law Uthman, became caliph (leader) in 644 but was assassinated in 656.

At that critical point, another of the Prophet's sons-in-law, Ali, became caliph. However, Muhammad's cousin Muawiya contested Ali's ascendancy, and when the two could not work out their differences peaceably, they went to war. In the Battle of Siffin in 657, the two sides fought to what appeared to be a draw. Considering this unexpected outcome, Ali and Muawiya agreed to allow a panel of widely respected Muslims to choose which leader should become caliph.

The problem was that a small but vocal group of Ali's supporters were upset that he had agreed to compromise instead of fighting to the bitter end. Claiming that he was not a true Muslim, they left the ummah and established their own version of Islam. This earned them the name Kharijites, meaning "those who left" in Arabic. Seeing them as troublemakers undermining his authority, Ali came out against the Kharijites and engaged them in battle the following year. Although he delivered them a major defeat, some of them survived and continued to resist both Ali and Muawiya. In 661 a Kharijite murdered Ali, which resulted in Muawiya becoming the undisputed caliph—except among the Kharijites.

> *"Take away the controversial teachings of arrogance, divisions, and hatreds which have badly infected our hearts."[1]*
>
> —From a popular Muslim prayer

Seeking Order and Meaning In Life

In the centuries that followed, the Kharijites remained an ever-present minority within Islam, opposing virtually all the caliphs and accusing them of not being conservative or devout enough. The descendants of these protesters within the ummah still exist today. Dwelling mainly in North Africa and Oman in southeastern Arabia, they reject the name Kharijite and call themselves the Ibadi.

The fact that many moderate Muslims have described members of the terrorist group ISIS as modern-day Kharijites stems from some striking similarities between the two groups. Among them are condemning other Muslims and killing anyone, including children and women, to further their cause. In 2014 prominent Muslim scholar Abdul-Aziz ibn Abdullah Al ash-Sheikh called ISIS an outgrowth of the Kharijites who "believed that killing Muslims was not a crime, and we do not consider either of them Muslims."[2] Even leaders of the equally infamous Islamist terror group al Qaeda have compared ISIS to the Kharijites.

Thus, the Kharijites/Ibadi claim that mainstream Muslims are not true Muslims, while most Muslims similarly accuse the Ibadi of not being real Muslims. Yet lurking beneath the text of these accusations is the reality that all Muslims, regardless of their political and other differences, strongly adhere to the same basic beliefs and practices. Indeed, both Islamic and Western scholars have frequently described the extraordinary sameness and universality of Islamic worship itself. As Oxford University professor Tariq Ramadan phrases it, "Islam's unity arises from the fact that Muslims, be they Sunni, Shia, or Ibadi, and whatever culture—Arab, African, Asian, or Western—or trend of thought—literalist, traditionalist, reformer, mystic—agree on the fundamental principles of their religion. [They] also agree on its ritual practices and its essential obligations and prohibitions. So, Islam is one."[3]

> "[God] is close, very close, and . . . He hears and answers our prayers."[4]
>
> —Oxford University scholar Tariq Ramadan

This situation is very different from that of Christianity, whose close to forty thousand denominations often display a multitude of variations in basic beliefs and practices. For example, some Christians pray in church once a week; others pray either every day or only now and then at home or elsewhere; still others do not pray at all.

In marked contrast, without fail and all over the world, five times each day at roughly the same times of the day, and kneeling and bowing in exactly the same manner, the 1.8 billion individuals making up the modern ummah pray together. Ramadan, who is himself a Muslim, comments that these ritual prayers remind all Muslims "of God's presence." They indicate that "He is close, very close, and that He hears and answers our prayers. To pray is to give thanks and to draw closer to God."[4]

The total agreement on this point among Muslims everywhere demonstrates the remarkable unity of belief within a religion whose members often violently disagree on other matters. "Both ends and means," Ramadan says, "constantly oblige us to consider the ultimate meaning and superior goals of religious practice."[5] Without a basic faith in God, he adds, "all around us would be disarray and meaninglessness."[6] In this view, the powerful urge to ensure that life is ordered and meaningful is the driving force behind Islam's astonishing unity of belief and worship.

CHAPTER ONE

The Origins of Islam

The story of the initial rise of Islam, the world's second-largest religion, is fascinating and at times gripping. The faith appeared rather suddenly, in a mere twinkling of history's normally slow-moving eye, in the early seventh century CE. Another unexpected aspect of Islam's birth is that it took place in the arid deserts and mountains of southern Arabia, far from the most populous civilizations of that era—in Europe, India, and China.

When viewing the history of their faith, many devout Muslims call the period predating Islam's rise the Jahiliyyah, or "Time of Ignorance." In this view, which is part of classic Islamic tradition, it was an age of religious confusion, the worship of multiple gods, social discord, and moral decadence. Then, like a bolt of cleansing lightning from on high, the Prophet Muhammad emerged and showed people the righteous qualities of belief in the single deity called Allah. In short order, the founding of Islam put an end to the Time of Ignorance.

The Pre-Islamic Arabian Religious Scene

Modern historians describe largely the same events except that they present those events in a less poetic and moralistic manner, as well as in more specific detail. The historians have found that the history of the pre-Islamic age was "far more complex than this tradition suggests," noted scholar of religions Reza Aslan explains.

> When referring to the religious experience of the pre-Islamic Arabs, it is important to make a distinction between the nomadic Bedouin who wandered through the Arabian deserts and the sedentary [stationary] tribes that

had settled in major [towns] like Mecca. [The] nomadic life-style is one that requires a religion to address immediate concerns: Which god can lead us to water? Which god can heal our illnesses?[7]

In contrast, the multiple gods worshipped in Arabian towns like Mecca were seen as mediators between humans and a more powerful creator God known as Allah, who was seen as a remote deity that took little direct interest in humanity. "Only in times of great peril," Aslan goes on, "would anyone bother consulting him. Otherwise, it was far more expedient to turn to the lesser, more accessible gods." These were the deities to whom the city Arabs prayed "when they needed rain, when their children were ill, [and] when they entered into battle."[8]

Those local Arabian gods were not the only ones the pre-Islamic Arabs worshipped. Small groups of peoples from foreign lands had settled in the region in recent centuries, including Jews, Christians, and Zoroastrian Persians. The three groups were strict

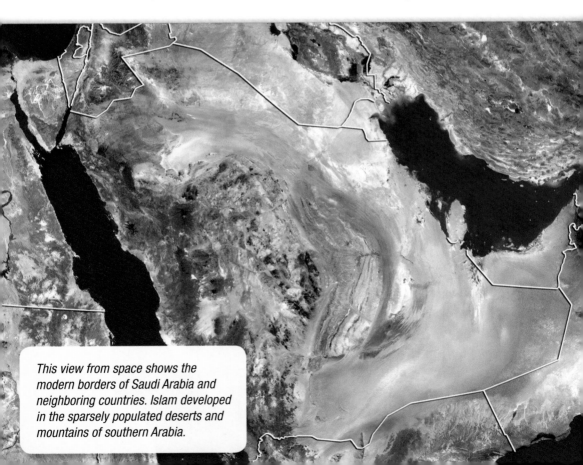

This view from space shows the modern borders of Saudi Arabia and neighboring countries. Islam developed in the sparsely populated deserts and mountains of southern Arabia.

monotheists—believers in a single God. That concept was similar to the Arab belief in Allah as the supreme God, only without the lesser gods the Arabs then revered. This shows that the Arabs of that era had already been exposed to the idea of a single God before Muhammad came on the scene. Indeed, some modern experts think that Muhammad's contact with local Arabian Jews and Christians may have partly inspired his vision of Allah as a sole deity with no other divinities mediating for him with humans.

Whichever gods the Arabs worshipped—whether those of the Bedouins or those of the city Arabs—no one claimed that the deities worshipped by others did not exist. Instead, the general view was that all of these gods were real. Moreover, to pay those diverse divinities a sort of collective respect, believers from all over Arabia went on a yearly pilgrimage to Mecca. Called the hajj, it was a custom that Muhammad and other Muslims would later tailor to fit their own needs.

The believers who went on those pre-Islamic pilgrimages ended their journeys in the center of Mecca at a cube-shaped structure known as the Kaaba. Both Muslim and non-Muslim scholars think that this was the spot where a meteorite had crashed to earth centuries before. The pre-Islamic Kaaba was decorated with statues of the many different gods then worshipped, and the pilgrims prayed to these idols during their stay in Mecca. Meanwhile, local officials saw an opportunity to make extra money. They charged the pilgrims a fee for the right to gaze on and kneel before the divine images.

From Orphaned Boy to Successful Merchant

This was the social and religious culture in which Muhammad, whose name means "worthy of praise," grew up. He was a member of the Quraysh, one of the many Arabian tribes of that time, each of which was a large kinship group consisting of hundreds or even thousands of individuals. Islamic tradition claims that he was forty when, in the year 610, he had the first of several divinely inspired visions that would radically alter his own society and eventually many others around the world.

Not much is known about Muhammad's life before that fateful year. Tradition holds that he was born in about 570 CE. Noted scholar of Islam Paul Grieve briefly summarizes some of the few other traditions about the faith's founder that later historians compiled. "Muhammad had almost no family from a very early age," he writes. "His father died before he was born, his mother when he was six, and his grandfather and guardian two years later."[9] When the boy was nine, his uncle, a trader named Abu Talib, took him in. Later, as an adult, Muhammad became a merchant too, probably because in that place and time there were few other ways to make a decent living. Grieve continues,

> Muhammad's options were limited. In the city of Mecca, surrounded by forbidding hills of untellable granite, there was no route to prosperity other than through trade. But Muhammad didn't have sufficient capital [money] to become a trader in his own right. [His] solution was to marry Khadijah, probably in 595 CE, when he was twenty-five years old and she was ten or more years older. Khadijah was both divorced and widowed [and] an independent woman of property, [and] the partnership with Muhammad prospered for the next fifteen years.[10]

Almost nothing is known about Muhammad's travels and dealings as a merchant during those fifteen years. More certain is that he was widely viewed as an honest man and that he had six children with Khadijah—two boys who died young and four girls who survived into adulthood. The couple named the four girls Zaynab, Fatima, Ruqayya, and Umm Kulthum.

The Astonishing Encounter in the Cave

The phenomenal visions that changed Muhammad's life and that of his family, neighbors, and millions yet unborn occurred when, at age forty, he was on an outing in the countryside near Mecca. It was common in the local society for grown men of all ages to occasionally hike alone into the wilderness to relax and meditate. On this particular trip, Muhammad climbed partway up the side of Mount Hira, then about 2 miles (3.2 km) from Mecca. There he came upon

The Battle of Badr, fought in 624 between the Muslims and the Meccans who opposed Islam, was an important event in the faith's early years for two reasons. First, it was the Muslims' first major military win. Moreover, it established in their minds that God had guided them to victory and was therefore on their side and desired to see Islam become successful. A verse from the Quran recalls that critical spiritual revelation: "You did not slay them, but it was Allah who slew them, and you did not smite [strike] when you smote [struck] the enemy, but it was Allah who smote, and that He might confer upon the believers a good gift from Himself; surely Allah is [all] hearing, knowing."

The fight at Badr was also significant because an incident that occurred before the battle revealed Muhammad's strength and flexibility as a military commander. The Muslims camped near the smallest of the few wells that existed in the region. Seeing this, one of Muhammad's companions, Hubab ibn al-Mundhir, asked the Prophet for permission to suggest a better plan. Muhammad immediately listened to and adopted the man's idea, which was to camp beside a larger well situated close to the Meccans' camp. Al-Mundhir correctly surmised that this would deprive the enemy of its chief source of water. According to Muslim scholar Tariq Ramadan, the incident shows that as a leader, Muhammad was not an autocrat, or dictator. Instead, he was "always offering his companions an essential role in consultation."

Quran 8:17.

Tariq Ramadan, *Introduction to Islam*. New York: Oxford University Press, 2017, p. 144.

a small cave, lay down inside, and fell asleep. Aslan colorfully describes what, according to Islamic tradition, happened next:

> Suddenly an invisible presence crushed him in its embrace. He struggled to break free but could not move. He was overwhelmed by darkness. The pressure in his chest increased until he could no longer breathe. He thought he was dying. As he surrendered his final breath, light and a terrifying voice washed over him like the break of dawn. "Recite," the voice commanded. "What shall I recite?" Muhammad gasped. The invisible presence tightened its embrace. "Recite!" "What shall I recite?" Muhammad asked again, his chest caving in.[11]

It was at that moment, with the pressure on his chest seemingly about to kill him, that the terrified man felt the awful strain suddenly disappear. In an instant, Muhammad sensed words coming to him from an unknown source and seemingly imprinting themselves on his heart. "Recite in the name of your Lord who created humanity from a clot of congealed blood," the message began. "Recite, and your lord is Most Generous, who taught by the pen; taught humanity what it did not know."[12] The voice also ordered Muhammad to prostrate himself, or lie facedown on the ground, before his God.

It soon became clear to the dumbfounded man that the powerful presence that had embraced him and channeled to him those words from God was the angel Gabriel. That mystical being revealed that he, Muhammad, was Allah's final prophet, or messenger, and again told the man to recite. More words came

Muslim children in Malaysia read verses from the Quran. Muhammad was illiterate, so he did not write down what he said the angel Gabriel told him. Instead, he repeated the angel's words to friends, who later dictated them to scribes.

to Muhammad in the astonishing encounter, as well as in subsequent sessions he had with the angel in the months and years that followed. Little by little, the words and sentences that entered the man's mind increased in volume, creating a steadily growing narrative.

Muhammad did not write down these utterances, which he believed to be of divine origin, because he was illiterate, or unable to read and write. Instead, the man repeated the words to some friends. In turn, they later told them to some scribes, literate individuals who made and maintained written records. Over time, the narrative recited by Muhammad added up to a book-length text that came to be called the sacred Quran. (In Arabic, the word *quran* means "recitation.") The book includes a total of 114 chapters, called suras, each of which contains a number of verses, called *ayat*. There are 6,236 verses in all.

Persecution and the Hegira

The fact that Muhammad's close friends immediately believed his story about the angel in the cave partly explains why the new faith he began to establish grew so rapidly. Clearly, they saw him as an honest, decent man who was not given to lying or flights of fancy. They also knew that he was illiterate and largely uneducated and reasoned that he could not have invented the Quran's long, complex narrative on his own.

For these and perhaps other reasons, one by one Muhammad started to gain ardent followers. They included his wife, Khadijah; his ten-year-old cousin, Ali; his adopted son, Zaid; his friend Abu Bakr; and several other relatives and acquaintances. All of them willingly became Muslims, meaning followers of Islam, a term meaning "submission to God." They believed that Muhammad was indeed God's final prophet, and for that reason thereafter Muslims often referred to him as "the Prophet." By 619 possibly more than one thousand Meccans had converted to the new faith.

However, although Islam did grow quickly overall, its members encountered some formidable obstacles along the way. The first consisted of the reaction of a number of local Meccans who were extremely devout in their worship of the traditional multiple Arabian gods. These individuals had no problem with the Muslims' reverence for Allah. After all, they and other Arabs held that God in high esteem themselves.

What bothered these traditionalist Meccans was the Muslims' insistence that the other gods who had long been worshipped at the Kaaba were false. Allah was the sole and only God that existed, Muhammad and his followers claimed. The traditionalists viewed that belief as highly offensive, so they condemned Muhammad and other Muslims and urged other Meccans to do the same. The persecutors tried to paint the Prophet as "merely another soothsayer or sorcerer," Grieve explains. They charged that Muhammad was "inspired by jinn, or traditional desert devils." Also, his claims of being a prophet were "ridiculed as unsupported by any miracles. His real motivation was alleged to be the wealth and power which had been denied him during his previous career as a merchant."[13]

For these reasons, the Meccan Muslims found themselves the targets of scorn and discrimination. After they suffered a number of threats and assaults, some fled to other towns. However, Muhammad, Khadijah, and about seventy other Muslims remained in Mecca in hopes of convincing the persecutors to be more tolerant. In the three years that followed, those earnest efforts failed, the persecution intensified, and making matters worse, Khadijah and Muhammad's uncle, Abu Talib, both passed away.

Fearing for his remaining followers' safety, early in 622 Muhammad sent them all away to Medina, located about 215 miles (346 km) north of Mecca. The one exception was his dear friend Abu Bakr, who refused to leave his side. Learning that some local assassins had targeted them, the two men quietly left Mecca during the night of July 16, 622. As they hurried toward Medina, they constantly had to elude the killers, who had given chase.

Fortunately for Muhammad and Abu Bakr, they made it safely to Medina. Their historic escape to that city was thereafter called the hegira, meaning "flight" in Arabic. It became a landmark in Islamic history, in part because it saved Muhammad's life and thereby allowed him to continue building and shaping the new faith he had established.

From War to Peace
Once Muhammad and his followers were comfortably settled in Medina, Islam continued to grow steadily. The faith gained many

Shortly before he passed away on June 8, 632 CE, Muhammad sat on a camel before a large crowd of followers and delivered what later came to be known as his last sermon. He said in part:

> O Men, listen to my words, for I do not know whether I shall meet you again on such an occasion in the future. O Men, your lives and your property shall be inviolate [undisturbed] until you meet your Lord. . . . Remember that you will indeed meet your Lord, and that He will indeed reckon your deeds. . . . O Men, the devil has lost all hope of ever being worshiped in this land of yours. Nevertheless, he is still anxious to determine the lesser of your deeds. Beware of him, therefore, for the safety of your religion. . . . O Men, a right belongs to you with respect to your women, and to your women a right with respect to you. It is your right that they not fraternize with anyone of whom you do not approve, as well as never to commit adultery. . . . Do treat your women well and be kind to them, for they are your partners and committed helpers. . . . O Men, hearken well to my words. Learn that every Muslim is a brother to every Muslim and that the Muslims constitute one brotherhood.

Quoted in Paul Grieve, *Islam: History, Faith, and Politics: The Complete Introduction.* New York: Carroll and Graf, 2006, pp. 135–36.

new converts, in part because to numerous Arab farmers and traders of that time and place, it was appealing for its relative simplicity. It required only a few straightforward obligations of its adherents. The primary ones were recognizing that only one God existed, praying to that deity five times each day, fasting during one month each year, and giving charity to the poor.

Building on the basic appeal of Islamic belief and practices, Muhammad wisely took several actions intended to maintain the faith's ongoing growth. In a bold move, for example, he had some scribes create a document that later came to be known as the Charter of Medina. It called for all citizens to pay taxes to support the community and ensured religious freedom for Jews, Christians, and other non-Muslims. According to University of Edinburgh scholar Carole Hillenbrand, "This document reveals

Muhammad's great skills as an arbitrator [negotiator] and his attempts to weld the wildly different elements of Medinan society into a unified community. He needed to establish a social order to give him and his followers vital protection in a new environment and to prevent civic unrest in Medina."[14]

Muhammad also assumed the responsibility of becoming a military commander in order to protect the city from attack. He knew that the Meccans still viewed Islam as a threat to the traditional Arabian religion and suspected that Mecca would soon launch an offensive against Medina to wipe out the Muslims there. To prevent such an assault from occurring, Muhammad decided to strike first. In 624 his followers attacked a Meccan trading caravan guarded by many Meccan soldiers. Soon afterward, the Muslims won their first full-fledged battle, at Badr, on the coast road leading northward toward Syria. There a mere three hundred of Muhammad's followers soundly defeated more than one thousand Meccans.

> "[Muhammad established] a social order to give him and his followers vital protection in a new environment."[14]
>
> —University of Edinburgh professor Carole Hillenbrand

The following year the angry Meccans struck back. In the Battle of Uhud, Mecca's army, numbering some three thousand men, clashed with about seven hundred Muslims. Many of the latter heard a report that Muhammad had been killed in the fighting, so they left the field. In reality, the Prophet had only been wounded. Although the retreat of his forces was embarrassing, Muhammad rightly reasoned that the skirmish had no clear winner, and the political and military status quo remained the same.

The fighting between the two cities went on for a few more years. Finally, in about 629 they signed a peace treaty. One of its provisions was that the Muslims were to be allowed to enter Mecca and pray at the Kaaba. As Muhammad had foreseen, their access to the city allowed them to steadily convert the rest of the population. The following year many of the Muslims in Medina moved back to Mecca. Moreover, once all the Meccan authorities

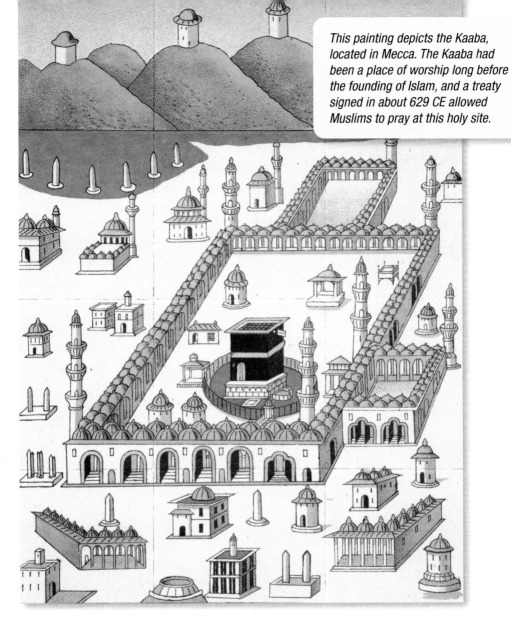

This painting depicts the Kaaba, located in Mecca. The Kaaba had been a place of worship long before the founding of Islam, and a treaty signed in about 629 CE allowed Muslims to pray at this holy site.

had converted to Islam, they ordered the Kaaba to be stripped of the statues of the old Arabic gods.

The Founder Passes On

Not long after this successful chain of events for the Muslims, they endured a much sadder experience. On June 8, 632, Muhammad died in Medina at age sixty-three. The exact cause is unknown. But based on the symptoms described by people close to him, modern medical experts say it might have been bacterial meningitis, an inflammation of the membranes surrounding the brain and spinal cord.

After confirming that the Prophet was dead, Abu Bakr assembled as many of the faithful as were near and shouted, "If anyone worships Muhammad, Muhammad is dead! If anyone worships God, God is alive and immortal!"[15] This was his way of reminding the faithful that as great as their leader had been, he was only a mortal man, whereas God, who had inspired Muhammad, was eternal. Those present at that moment naturally wanted to ensure that the ummah would survive and prosper, even without the founder. Surely, they could not have imagined that their then humble congregation would, in the fullness of time, grow into a religious community numbering more than 1 billion believers.

CHAPTER TWO

What Do Muslims Believe?

In the year 632 the news of Muhammad's untimely passing shocked and saddened all his followers. Yet although the man who had established their faith was gone, they managed to keep on functioning as a religious unit. Moreover, as it had in the past, Islam continued to steadily draw new converts.

This survival of the faith was in large degree the result of the simple, firm, and workable basic beliefs that Muhammad had early on established for the ummah. The most fundamental and essential of all those beliefs was the concept of God that the Prophet had introduced. In pre-Islamic Arabia, Allah had been seen as the creator deity. Islam retained that vision but added to it the idea that God has no divine competition. He is the only God that exists, Muhammad said, and he is all-powerful and knows about everything that happens on earth and among humans. These concepts appear in the Quran's twentieth sura, which states in part that God is "He who created the earth and the high heavens. The Most Merciful; on the Throne [of heaven] He settled. To Him belongs everything in the heavens and the earth, and everything between them, and everything beneath the soil. If you speak aloud—He knows the secret, and the most hidden."[16]

The Quran, which Muslims believe Muhammad revealed to humanity a bit at a time, addresses some of these same ideas somewhat differently in the second sura, in what is often called the Throne Verse. "Whatever is in the heavens and whatever is in the Earth," it asserts, belongs to God, who maintains the greatest of all thrones. As for the humans God created, "He knows what is before them and what is behind them, and they

21

cannot comprehend anything out of His knowledge except what He pleases. His knowledge extends over the heavens and the earth, and the preservation of them both tires Him not, and He is the Most High, the Great."[17]

The Sacred Quran

A second fundamental Islamic belief consists of the Quran itself. For Muslims, that book—or narrative, list of verses, or whatever one chooses to call it—is more than a collection of religious sayings and rules. All members of Islam view the Quran literally as words and principles passed directly from God to Muhammad through an intermediary being—the angel Gabriel. As a compilation of God's words, therefore, to Muslims the Quran is both sacred and flawless.

At first the Quran's contents spread from one person to another orally. Later, at the orders of Muhammad's initial successor, Abu Bakr, all portions of the Islamic scripture were committed to writing. In those days there were no printing presses, so each version of the Quran had to be painstakingly copied by hand. That meant that the number of complete copies was limited. As a result, it became common for those fortunate enough to own a copy to read its verses to others, some of whom memorized it.

"Muham-mad's minis-try and the message of the Quran, as the Last of the Last, now represents God's final word."[18]

—Expert on Islam Paul Grieve

Partly because Muslims through the centuries have believed the Quran to contain God's own words, it was and remains a major source of moral guidance for the faithful. Furthermore, they see the document as a veritable font of religious rules and legal precepts. Also, and very importantly, Muslims insist that the Quran contains not only God's own sayings, but his final sayings to humanity. Muslims believe that "God has sent many messengers before Mohammad to guide mankind," Paul Grieve explains. "And the lives of a few are recounted in some detail" in the Quran. "But God's messengers have been ignored, or their warnings perverted to some human end. Muhammad's ministry and the

The Arabic characters adorning the horse in this painting comprise what is known as the Throne Verse in the Quran, which asserts the supremacy of God over all humans and the earth.

message of the Quran, as the Last of the Last, now represents God's final word, which man ignores at his peril."[18]

In addition, Muslims tend to view the original Arabic version of the Quran as more precise than even the best of its translations into other languages. Supposedly, God and Gabriel had presented its words to Muhammad in Arabic. Therefore, the exact meanings of its words and phrases are more fully understandable in that tongue. This is why Muslims see the Quran's Arabic edition as overall superior to the other versions.

Angels, Satan, and Unbelievers

Gabriel's role in giving Muhammed the Quranic text was part of another basic Islamic precept—belief in angels. In Islam, an angel, or *malak* in Arabic, is a messenger or intermediary between God and humanity, as Gabriel was between Allah and Muhammad. According to Islamic belief, God created both angels and humans to serve him.

But there was, and remains, a significant difference between the two groups. Namely, God gave people free will, which means that they can choose to either believe or not believe in God. In

Along with Moses, Jesus, and other important Judeo-Christian figures, the Quran devotes an unusually large amount of space to Jesus's mother, Mary. Held in extremely high esteem by Muslims through the ages, she is the only woman mentioned by name in that document.

Some of the details about Mary in the Quran are very similar to those in the Bible. For instance, in both holy writings God sends an angel to her to announce that she will soon give birth to a special child (an episode often called the Annunciation). However, other details about Mary in the Quran are unique to that book, including the episode in which Jesus is born. As University of Edinburgh scholar Carole Hillenbrand tells it, when Mary realizes that she is about to give birth,

> she withdraws to a remote place where the pangs of childbirth drive her to the trunk of a palm tree. Overwhelmed by her pain, she cries out, "I wish I had died and been forgotten long before this!" (Quran 9.23) Then the baby Jesus speaks to her, saying that she should not be sad; he points to a stream that God had placed below her, and tells her to shake the palm tree, and dates will fall upon her. Thus she is miraculously provided by God with food and water. Mary then returns to her people carrying the child.

Carole Hillenbrand, *Introduction to Islam.* New York: Thames and Hudson, 2015, p. 73.

contrast, Muslims hold, angels have no free will. Those divine messengers are incapable of committing sins and automatically carry out God's orders. Angels' duties typically include observing human society, keeping track of both good deeds and sins that people commit, and guiding human souls to heaven or hell after death.

There was one angel who did not follow God's orders, however, according to Islamic belief. His name was Satan. Considering humans to be ultimately superior to angels, God ordered his angels to prostrate themselves, or bow down, before the first man, Adam. But Satan, thinking himself superior rather than inferior to people, refused. As told in the Quran:

Your Lord said to the angels, "I am creating a human being from clay. When I have formed him, and breathed into him of My spirit, fall prostrate before him. So the angels fell prostrate, all of them. Except for Satan. He was too proud, and one of the faithless. [God] said, "O Satan, what prevented you from prostrating before what I created with My Own hands? Are you too proud, or were you one of the exalted?" [Satan] said, "I am better than he; You created me from fire, and You created him from clay." [God] said, "Then get out of here! You are an outcast! And My curse will be upon you until the Day of Judgment."[19]

The way God treated Satan for his insolence, Muslims believe, is similar to how God deals with unbelievers (or disbelievers)—those who refuse to accept God and his rules. Their fate is also laid out in the Quran:

Those who disbelieve, and hinder from the path of God, and oppose the Messenger after guidance has become clear to them—they will not hurt God in the least, but He will nullify their deeds. O you who believe! Obey God, and obey the Messenger, and do not let your deeds go to waste. Those who disbelieve, and hinder from God's path, and then die as disbelievers—God will not forgive them.[20]

Heaven, Hell, and Judgment Day

Most Muslims agree that the people whom God does not forgive, for one reason or another, end up with Satan in hell. As described in the Quran, it is an awful place very similar to classic medieval Christian visions of it. Those who dare to disbelieve God's existence or disobey his rules will be forced to wear "a garment of fire," the Quran states. In addition, "over their heads will be poured out boiling water. With it will be scalded what is within their bodies, as well as their skins. In addition there will be maces of iron to punish them. Every time they wish to get away [from them due to extreme] anguish, they will be forced back."[21]

Those humans who do believe in God, by contrast, are destined for heaven after they die, Muslims believe. The Quran's ninth sura mentions the faithful arriving in beautiful "gardens of everlasting bliss."[22] Another sacred verse tells how those entering heaven will be greeted by their family members who have passed on before them. There will also be angels on hand to greet the entrants: "Angels shall enter from every gate with the salutation: 'Peace be with you, that you persevered in patience! Now how excellent is the final home!'"[23]

Whether it will be sent to hell or to heaven, every human soul, according to the Islamic belief system, must first be judged by God. There are several different descriptive terms for Judgment Day in the Quran and other Islamic writings. These names include the Day of Reckoning, the Day of Decision, the Hour, the Last Day, the Day of Resurrection, and the Day of Assembling. Whatever one chooses to call it, on that day people's souls will rise up from their graves. With a wave of his hand, God will gather them together in their countless billions.

God will then proceed to weigh the souls' good deeds and bad deeds committed when they were living on earth. In doing so, he will consult the so-called Book of Deeds, an ongoing tally of human actions that he set in motion at the dawn of human existence. After human souls are split into "good" and "bad" groups, the good ones will gather on God's right side and from there move into heaven; the other group, pushed to his left side, will be dragged away by demons into hell's fiery depths. The Quran does not specify when Judgment Day will occur, and numerous religious leaders, writers, and others have made educated and noneducated guesses on that point over the years.

> "The Quran is the third of the line of monotheistic revelations, coming as it does after the Old and New Testaments."[24]
>
> —Scholar Carole Hillenbrand

A Long Line of Prophets

The similarities between the Islamic and Christian concepts of sin, divine judgment, heaven, and hell are not accidental. As Carole Hillenbrand points out, "the Quran is the third of the line of monotheistic revelations, coming as it does after the Old and New Testaments,"[24] the major Jewish scripture and the major Christian one. In fact, Muhammad and the early Muslims were well aware that their faith was closely related to Judaism and Christianity. Islam refers to Muslims, Jews, and Christians together as the venerable People of the Book—that is, part of the same monotheistic lineage that began long ago with a man named Abraham.

Abraham was in a sense the father of all three faiths and as such is seen by Muslims as an important early prophet, or messenger of God. Excluding Muhammad, the Quran mentions close to thirty prophets following Abraham. Several of these messengers appear in the Bible's Old and New Testaments, including Ishmael, Isaac, Noah, Moses, Job, Solomon, David, and Jesus. Muhammad, of course, was the last prophet, according to Islamic belief. The central message of all the prophets, Muslims think, was that there is but one God and to warn people that they must follow that deity or else face eternal punishment on Judgment Day.

A clear example of this belief is Jesus. Although Muslims revere him as one of their prophets, they think that, like Muhammad and the others, he was not divine himself but rather a divinely approved messenger. In the Islamic view, Jesus did not die on the cross; instead, he escaped crucifixion, and God took him straight to heaven. Meanwhile, a man who looked like Jesus was crucified outside Jerusalem's walls.

> *"[Jesus] will speak to the people from the crib, and in adulthood, and will be one of the righteous."*[25]
>
> —The Quran

Most importantly, the Islamic version of Jesus admonished people to believe in the one God and follow that God's rules. The Quran states that Jesus "will speak to the people from the crib, and in adulthood, and will be one of the righteous."[25] Another

In this painting from sixteenth-century Turkey, Jesus is depicted as being taken to heaven by angels from a minaret at the mosque in Damascus. Muslims believe that Jesus did not die on the cross but was taken directly to heaven, while someone who resembled him was crucified.

passage confirms that Jesus did perform various miracles and quotes him as saying,

I have come to you with a sign from your Lord. I make for you out of clay the figure of a bird; then I breathe into it, and it becomes a bird by God's leave. And I heal the blind and the leprous, and I revive the dead, by God's leave. And [I came] to make lawful for you some of what was forbidden to you. I have come to you with a sign from your Lord; so fear God [and] worship Him. That is a straight path.[26]

The Rift Between Sunni and Shia

Beliefs such as recognition that there is a single God and that Muhammad was that deity's final prophet, along with Islamic visions of heaven and hell, were and remain central to the faith itself. They were set down in the Quran, and no Muslim is allowed to question them. In contrast, a few human-generated beliefs developed among the faithful after Muhammad's passing.

The Sufis' Mystical Beliefs

The Sunnis and Shias are the largest but not the only distinct groups within Islam. One of the others consists of the practioners of Sufism. The Sufis, who make up about 4 to 5 percent of Muslims worldwide, bring a mystical quality to Islamic beliefs and worship because their central goal is to discover the truth of God's knowledge and love through direct personal experience of God. They call their search for that experience "ascending degrees of illumination." If they are fortunate enough to actually commune with the divine, or at least experience what they believe is real contact with the Creator, they can achieve *fana*, which they describe as a state of being intoxicated, or high, on heavenly love.

In the quest for this wonderful experience, a Sufi consults the Quran and picks out verses that appear open to multiple interpretations. He or she then studies those sections over and over, trying to glean from them meanings that touch him or her personally. Much of this spiritual searching, Sufis believe, involves the soul. Most mainstream Muslims view the soul as a material substance connected somehow to the body. In comparison, the Sufis see the soul as a more intangible essence that is separate from the body and linked in some mysterious way to God. In death, a Sufi believes, his or her soul will be reabsorbed into the divine spirit from which it originated.

Chief among these are the heartfelt convictions surrounding the breach between Islam's two principal subdivisions—Sunni and Shia. Their differences were at first political and social, and to some degree still are. Over time, however, they also developed into a genuine and deep division in theological belief.

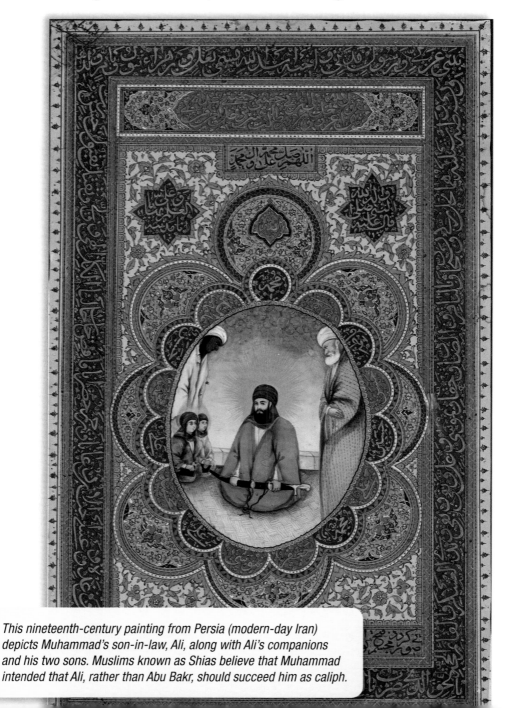

This nineteenth-century painting from Persia (modern-day Iran) depicts Muhammad's son-in-law, Ali, along with Ali's companions and his two sons. Muslims known as Shias believe that Muhammad intended that Ali, rather than Abu Bakr, should succeed him as caliph.

That division originated with the issue of who should take Muhammad's place as leader of the ummah following his death in 632. When the Prophet's close companion, Abu Bakr, succeeded him as caliph, the bulk of the Muslim community agreed that Abu Bakr was a capable leader. The problem was that a minority of Muslims felt that Muhammad's son-in-law and cousin, Ali, was the rightful caliph. Those who backed Abu Bakr and his successors later became known as Sunni Muslims, or Sunnis; those who supported Ali and his successors became known as Shia Muslims, or Shias.

Early on, both sides insisted they had evidence to back up their claims. Shias, for instance, pointed out that during Muhammad's last hajj, he publicly proclaimed Ali to be the ummah's spiritual guide. So, they reasoned, only Ali and his successors should lead Islam ever after. The Sunnis, in comparison, argued that when the Prophet lay on his deathbed, he selected Abu Bakr ~~~ the community in prayer, and that implied Muhammad desired Abu Bakr to be the next caliph.

These initially political differences between the Sunnis and Shias may seem trivial to many modern non-Muslims. But to the Sunnis and Shias themselves, they are fundamental and momentous. Grieve ably explains this rift in belief by summarizing the Shias' argument:

> God continued to convey His divine will to humans even after the last words of the Quran had been received by Muhammad. In place of the "corrupt" Sunni caliphate line, Shia regard Ali as the first of a line of twelve imams [spiritual leaders], sent by God to interpret and direct [social and political events] following the death of the Prophet. Thus, the Shia imams, like the Catholic popes making [church law over time], built up a body of "unerring" Shia law that diverges from the Sunni-based interpretation of mainstream Sunni Islam.[27]

Today more than 80 percent of Muslims are Sunni; while around 10 percent are Shia. Although members of both groups revere the Quran and follow basic Islamic practices, they still often distrust and denounce each other. They also frequently take opposing political sides and at times engage in violent strife. The leaders of Saudi Arabia, who control Islam's holiest shrines at Mecca and Medina, are Sunnis. In contrast, the leading Shia power in the Middle East is Iran, which sees the Saudi regime as an enemy. These and other Sunni- and Shia-dominated nations typically take opposite sides in regional conflicts. Particularly bloody is the civil war in Syria. There the Shia minority, led by the country's president, Bashar al-Assad, opposes rebels representing the nation's Sunni majority.

The bitter opposition between the Sunnis and Shias over past events they see as pivotal to their faith is in a sense comparable to the unwavering devotion of all Muslims to the Quran. Both clearly illustrate how passionate the followers of Islam are about their beliefs, even when those beliefs clash with those of other Muslims.

CHAPTER THREE

How Do Muslims Practice Their Faith?

As is true of the followers of all religions, Muslims have practices, or rituals, that they follow daily, monthly, or yearly as expressions of their faith in God. There are Islamic rituals commonly associated with the birth of children, for example, with marriage and weddings, and with death and burial. These sorts of everyday practices often vary in nature somewhat from one country or region to another within the greater global Islamic community.

Far fewer variations exist, however, among Islam's core practices, which Muslims everywhere perform either regularly or at certain times in their lives. These central rituals are known as the Five Pillars. "More than anything," Reza Aslan comments,

> the Five Pillars are meant as a metaphor for [symbol of] Islam. They are a summary not just of what is required to be a member of the ummah, but also of what it means to be a Muslim. Contrary to perception, the Pillars are not oppressive obligations—quite the opposite. These are highly pragmatic [practical] rituals, in that the believer is responsible only for those tasks that he or she is able to perform.[28]

Aslan's last point is important. It emphasizes that in Islam God expects believers to perform all the pillars only if a person is physically able to do so. If disease, extreme poverty, or some other factor keeps the person from doing one or two of these rituals, God understands and overlooks the omissions.

The Secrets of the Heart

The first of the Five Pillars, the *shahada*, is a general statement of belief. It is "the first conscious act by which a woman or a man becomes a Muslim,"[29] Tariq Ramadan explains. (This and the other major Islamic pillars are described here as performed by the Sunnis, who make up the majority of Muslims. The Shias, Sufis, and other smaller Islamic groups perform the pillars with only a few minor variations.)

This statement of faith in God, which is most often recited during prayer, consists in part of an oath or pledge containing words to the effect of "I bear witness that there is no god worthy of worship except Allah and that Muhammad is the Messenger of Allah."[30] One is expected to recite this pledge at least once in one's lifetime, but some Muslims repeat it periodically to show their respect for God. When possible, a person says the words in Arabic, since that was the language that Muhammad spoke. By custom, also when possible, he or she does so in front of two or more witnesses.

Nevertheless, the particular language employed and the presence of witnesses are not absolute necessities, because the shahada is most of all a private interaction between a person and God. According to Ramadan, "Once a person has pronounced the attestation of faith and considers her- or himself a Muslim, no one has the right to challenge that decision or to exclude or remove that person from Islam. A religious institution may rule upon actions or words as not conforming to the creed and principles of Islam, but no authority can rule upon faith and the secrets of the heart."[31]

> *"No authority can rule upon [a Muslim's] faith and the secrets of the heart."*[31]
>
> —Oxford University professor Tariq Ramadan

The Leveling Experience of Prayer

Islam's second major pillar of practice is *salah*, or prayer. Muslims are expected to pray five times a day no matter where they may be or what they may be doing, unless they are physically prevented from doing so. The fact that Muslims pray so often reflects the importance of that spiritual practice, as Carole Hillenbrand explains:

According to a Muslim proverb, "To pray and to be a Muslim are synonymous." And indeed, the sheer number of times that Muslims are required to pray every single day of the year make prayer the core ritual in their worship of God. They are regularly reminded of Him even in the hurly-burly of their daily lives. In the act of prayer they stop and reflect upon spiritual truths and their own commitment to God. Many recent converts to Islam comment on the way in which performing the ritual prayer five times a day gives structure and meaning to their lives.[32]

A Muslim man engages in salah, or prayer. Muslims are expected to pray five times a day, regardless of where they are or what they are doing.

Each time—or at least most times—a Muslim prays, beforehand he or she performs a related ritual: washing. In the context of religious practice, it is called *wudhu*. In large part because Muhammad long ago emphasized that Muslims should be clean when presenting themselves to God, worshippers usually follow a preset washing routine. They cleanse the right hand, and then the left, three times each. Then they wash the face, arms, hair, ears, and feet.

For a Muslim, another preparation for prayer is making sure that she or he is in the right frame of mind. The person tries to clear the mind of worries, family and social obligations, and other nonspiritual aspects of life and to concentrate solely on communing with God. Islamic belief holds that if a Muslim prays with an improper attitude, God will not credit him or her with having prayed. This reality is addressed in the Quranic verse that states, "Woe to those who pray, but are unmindful of their prayer, or who pray only to be seen by people."[33]

Muslims can pray anywhere, but it is thought to be especially good to pray with others in a mosque. Approaching God together in a congregation helps Muslims realize that all humanity is one, and all are equal in God's sight. Paul Grieve points out, "The defining characteristic of prayer in congregation is equality: from the [physical placement] of rich and poor side by side, right down to the last words, 'May the peace and forgiveness of God be upon you.' [That] greeting recognizes no rank and no hierarchy [ladder of authority]. Muslim prayers are a leveling experience, shoulder to shoulder without class or category."[34]

After preparations are completed, a person follows some physical rituals when performing the actual prayer, rituals originally established by Muhammad. First, he or she faces in the direction of Mecca, where the sacred Kaaba still rests. Then the worshipper executes a sequence of gestures and bodily movements, including momentarily placing his or her hands and forehead on the ground or floor. Having finished praying, the person goes about his or her business for a few hours until it is time to pray again.

However, when that time comes, that person and/or other Muslims might be immersed in work or other activities and not realize it is time for the next prayer. Fortunately for them, Islamic communities long ago instituted a custom to remind the faithful when prayer times are imminent. In most Muslim neighborhoods around the world, several times a day the *adhan*, or "call to prayer," is heard. It is most often performed by a *muezzin*, a representative of a local mosque. Almost always singing the message in a series of pleasing tones, the muezzin states the following words (translated here by Muslim educator Huda), or at least a very similar variation of them: "I bear witness that there is no god except the One God. I bear witness that Muhammad is the messenger of God. Hurry to the prayer. Hurry to success. God is Great. There is no god except the One God."[35]

Universal Standards of Muslim Prayer

When Muslims go to pray, they undergo a series of set, standard physical and verbal gestures. First the individuals praying face the direction of Mecca and say, "Allahu Akbar," meaning "God is great." At the same time, they raise their hands to about the level of their shoulders. Next they place their hands on their chest and recite one or more verses from the Quran. Then they bow from the waist (a move called *ruku*) and repeat "Glory be to God the most great" three times. After that they fall to their knees and place their palms, toes, and forehead on the floor or ground. After reciting some pious phrases in that position, they sit up for a few seconds before returning to the bowed position once more. As they go from one position to another, the individuals always repeat the words "God is great" before each move. As many Muslims do while praying, they may next sit up again and recite the statement of faith (Islam's First Pillar). Then, still sitting, they turn their head first toward the right and then toward the left, in each case saying, "Peace be upon you." That gesture is directed at the angels that Muslims believe are always hovering nearby. Although these movements and phrases are seen as minimal, Muslims can and sometimes do pray longer if they are moved to do so.

Quoted in BBC, "Muslim Prayer Movements." www.bbc.co.uk.

Helping the Poor and Needy

Islam's third pillar, called *zakat*, is the practice of giving charity to society's poorest and least fortunate individuals. This is a required act for Muslims, unlike charitable contributions among non-Muslims, which are voluntary. Typically, Muslims pay 2.5 percent of their personal cash wealth, or salary, per year to those in the community who are in need. Some Muslims, both rich ones and others of average means, choose to pay more than the minimum.

Not all Muslims are expected to pay zakat. For example, since this practice consists of aiding the poor, the poor themselves are exempt. Islamic authorities reckon a person's ability to pay zakat by determining whether he or she possesses the *nisab*, the minimum amount of wealth one must own to be duty bound to pay zakat. The nisab was originally calculated using gold or silver coins and still is in some places. Muslims in most industrialized countries, however, particularly in the West, determine the nisab by using their nation's official poverty line. Those whose yearly wealth is above that line must pay zakat, while those below the line are the recipients of that aid.

"Whatever good you do, God is aware of it."[36]

—The Quran

The official justifications for paying zakat in Islam are most often described as both societal and personal benefits. The most obvious benefit in the eyes of most Muslims is that those who give are obeying God. Among the Quran's several mentions of the obligation to pay zakat, one states, "They ask you what they [the faithful] should give. Say, 'Whatever charity you give is for the parents, and the relatives, and the orphans, and the poor, and the wayfarer.' Whatever good you do, God is aware of it."[36]

Another benefit of zakat frequently cited by Muslims is that it teaches people to practice self-discipline and not to hoard huge amounts of money they will never need. Behind that thought is the idea that no one can take their riches with them after they die; thus, there is no reason to cling to excess wealth. In theory, therefore, zakat helps a person free him- or herself from greed for money and possessions. Also, achieving this kind of freedom causes one to be honest with oneself, and those who are honest with themselves are more likely to be honest with others.

Fasting During Ramadan

Islam's fourth pillar is the *sawm*—the fast—which to some degree resembles the Christian custom of fasting during Lent. During the sawm Muslims refrain from eating, drinking any beverages, and in some cases smoking, sexual activity, and other activities from sunup to sundown during the holy month of Ramadan, which falls at different times during the secular calendar year.

By taking part in the fast, a Muslim demonstrates her or his appreciation to God for creating humans and for his bounty to them over the centuries. The worshipper also hopes to make up

A Muslim family in Istanbul makes a picnic of their evening meal during the holy month of Ramadan. Muslims are expected to fast from sunup to sundown during Ramadan.

for his or her past sins. There is another dimension to the sawm, however, that is no less crucial, as Grieve explains. One objective of the fast, he says, "is to diminish the believer's love for the world and reduce his or her dependence on material things."[37]

These motivations for the fast may at first glance make it sound grim and restrictive. In fact, however, Ramadan is a favorite and happy time of year for most Muslims. During the twenty-nine days of that month, families and communities celebrate in various ways. One highlight is *iftar*, the festive traditional evening meal that ends the fast for the day; another is *suhoor*, the pre-dawn meal that leads to the resumption of the fast for the following day.

Muslim Marriage and Divorce

In many countries, any couple that wants to get married, including two Muslims, must apply for a marriage license issued from a town or other official institution to make the marriage legally binding. However, Muslims everywhere consider the ceremony itself, which varies considerably from one Muslim culture to another, to be the real confirmation that they are legally married. A Muslim marriage is seen as a kind of social contract that ensures that the husband and wife owe certain obligations to each other. In many Muslim countries, if those obligations are not met, people view the contract to be broken, and the couple can get a divorce. However, in some other Muslim nations, divorce for any reason is frowned on. Also, in some Muslim cultures marriages arranged by fathers or other relatives are still common. Such unions are sometimes actually happy ones, even when the two people have never met before tying the knot. Islam allows a man to have up to four wives at one time. He must, however, be able to support them all in an equal degree of comfort, which will vary according to his income, and he cannot treat one better than the others. If he does, some or all have grounds for divorce. In contrast, Muslim women are not allowed to marry more than one man, primarily because it would be too hard to determine which husband fathered which child.

Engaging in fasting during Ramadan is not an absolutely rigid requirement of every single Muslim at all times. As in the cases of the faith's other pillars, Islamic authorities allow a bit of leeway to accommodate the realities of human life. For example, people who are physically or mentally ill are often excused from the fast. So are children younger than twelve, very elderly people, pregnant women, women who are breast-feeding or menstruating, and people in the midst of traveling to other countries. Nevertheless, adults who are excused from the fast for any of those reasons are expected to make up for it by fasting on some later date. One can also make a donation to the poor in lieu of fasting.

Islam's Most Majestic Practice

The fifth and last of Islam's traditional Five Pillars is the hajj, the journey to Mecca. That custom, borrowed from the pre-Islamic Arabians, acquired new meaning after Muhammad introduced the Islamic faith. Every Muslim who is physically and financially able to do so is required to embark on that sometimes arduous voyage at least once in his or her lifetime. In the process, the pilgrims feel "fully integrated into the worldwide community of Muslims,"[38] remarks scholar Neal Robinson.

Both during the journey and upon arriving in Mecca, the pilgrims usually follow a series of traditional customs that remain almost identical to those established in the early medieval period. Some of those rituals revolve around the manner in which the faithful personally approach this most physically demanding and majestic of Islam's major practices. According to the BBC's extensive website on Islam, for example, pilgrims on the hajj must enter *ihram*, a special state of ritual purity. People do this by

> wearing special white clothes (which are also called *ihram*) and obeying [several] regulations: The person on the Hajj may not engage in marital relations, shave or cut their nails, use cologne or scented oils, kill or hunt anything, fight or argue. Women must not cover their faces, even if they would do so in their home country. Men may not wear clothes with stitching. Bathing is allowed but scented soaps are frowned upon.[39]

Thousands of Muslims gather at the Kaaba during the hajj, or pilgrimage to Mecca. Every Muslim who is physically and financially able to do so is obligated to undertake this journey at least once in his or her lifetime.

The grand climax of the hajj occurs when the pilgrims enter the holiest of Islam's holy places—the heart of Mecca—and walk seven times around the Kaaba. This crucial act of the faith is called the *tawaf*. For those Muslims who take part in it, "the Ka'ba becomes the axis of the world," Aslan writes. Here, "*every* direction is the direction of prayer. It is, one might say, the centrifugal force of praying in the presence of the sacred shrine that compels the worshiper to orbit the sanctuary."[40] A man who completes the expedition of the hajj ever after bears the proud title of hajji. An equally proud woman who does so is known as a hajjah.

The Struggle for Piety

Although the Five Pillars are Islam's central and most critical rituals, a number of others exist. Of these, one of the more noteworthy is jihad, which some Muslims informally call the sixth pillar. Its literal meaning is "a struggle." The vast majority of Islamic scholars and ordinary Muslims see that struggle as a personal one. They generally define jihad as an attempt to find one's most truthful, worthwhile way in the world and, if possible, achieve moral excellence.

The chief aim of this kind of jihad is to do one's best to purify one's soul of harmful, unjust influences. In this sense it is in many ways a struggle to avoid sin and make one's soul as acceptable as possible to God. The Hadith—the collected sayings of Muhammad—contains various references to this kind of personal struggle. One states that it is righteous to put the cause of goodness and justice above even one's own family and worldly ambition. Another urges all "true" Muslims to strive toward good and constructive deeds. The Quran also contains such references to jihad as a personal struggle. One says, "You who believe! Stand out firmly for Allah's witnesses to fair dealing, and let not the hatred of others to you make you swerve to wrong and depart from justice. Be just: that is next to piety."[41] Another interpretation of jihad is a struggle for a just cause. It might be the cause of religious freedom or the attempt to free people from slavery. Yet it can also mean resorting to warfare to defend one's family, land, and/or rights. Over the centuries, a small minority of the faithful have twisted this definition of jihad to mean a so-called holy war against either non-Muslims or other Muslims. In recent times, the most notorious of these extremists have been members of the terrorist groups al Qaeda and ISIS.

In contrast, a majority of Muslims around the globe reject the violence of the extremists. To most of the faithful, jihad's personal struggle for excellence parallels the ways in which they strive to better themselves by fasting and giving to the poor. They argue that nearly all Islamic rituals are designed to show devotion to and humility before God. Indeed, says Hillenbrand, "to improve oneself spiritually is a struggle that has infused Muslim piety ever since the time of the Prophet."[42]

CHAPTER FOUR

Rules to Live By

In Islam many of the rules by which people live and govern themselves, including those that determine which social activities are acceptable or unacceptable, are recorded in the Quran. For instance, there are several references to drinking alcohol, a pastime most Muslims frown on. Various Quranic excerpts also set down rules about gambling, eating pork and certain other foods, and other forbidden activities.

By comparison, rules pertaining to when and how to celebrate various holidays are in large degree determined by the Islamic calendar. Its dates are labeled AH, which stands for *anno hijiri*, or "in the year of the hegira." Thus, "year one" in the Islamic calendar, or AH 1, was that in which Muhammad made his historic flight from Mecca to Medina. AH 1 is equivalent to the date 622 CE in the more universal BCE/CE dating system.

The Islamic calendar is lunar, or based on the moon's movements, like the traditional Jewish calendar. The Islamic version has twelve months, each consisting of twenty-nine or thirty days, rendering 354 days in all. Unlike the Jewish calendar, however, the Islamic one possesses no built-in system designed to make it match, over time, the solar calendar used almost universally around the globe. As a result, the Islamic calendar falls behind the solar one slightly as time goes on, and Muslim holidays take place on different dates in succeeding years. After a period of a little more than thirty-two years, the Islamic calendar catches up with itself and starts to repeat the same cycle of dates.

Most modern Muslim countries are aware that this lunar dating system is outmoded and awkward in certain ways. Therefore, they use it mainly for religious purposes, including reckoning dates for holidays, to show respect for God and tradition. Meanwhile, to better adjust to the needs of modern life, they employ the Gregorian solar calendar for affairs of state, commercial endeavors, agriculture, and other secular activities.

Two Key Holy Feasts

With their dates marked plainly on the lunar calendar, the various Islamic holidays are highly anticipated times of the year for Muslims. Many of the religious rules modern Muslims are expected to follow revolve around these holidays. Moreover, Muslims are expected to celebrate the major annual holy days unless they are too ill to do so. Simply observing these holidays, therefore, is seen as a major religious rule in Islam.

Like Christmas among Christians and Passover among Jews, the main Muslim holidays combine religious piety and observance with feasting and other joyous festivities. A notable example is Islam's principal feast day, Eid al-Adha, or the Feast of Sacrifice (also called the Day of Sacrifice). It takes place during the twelfth month of the Islamic year—Dhu al-Hijjah. This holiday also occurs at the same time as the conclusion of the hajj—the annual pilgrimage to Mecca.

Indeed, the hajj is part of the series of ancient events this holiday commemorates. First, the prophet Abraham (Ibrahim in Arabic) and his sons arrived in Mecca. There God ordered Abraham to sacrifice, or ritually kill, his son Ishmael. (In the Old Testament, revered by Jews and Christians, God told Abraham to sacrifice his other son, Isaac.) Although horrified and reluctant, Abraham was about to obey this order when at the last minute God rescinded it and allowed the boy to live.

After that, in Islamic lore, the father and son erected the Kaaba, history's first house of worship. According to a verse in the Quran, God said, "Remember Ibrahim and Ishmael raised the foundations of the House with this prayer: 'Our Lord! Accept this service from us, for you are the All-Hearing, the All-Knowing.'"[43] (Islamic tradition holds that Adam built the first version of the Kaaba, but it was destroyed in the Great Flood, and Abraham and Ishmael rebuilt it.) Finally, Abraham established the hajj, and Ishmael went on to father the Arabic race.

Muslims view these events, especially Ishmael's near sacrifice, as a historic example of a person's steadfast faith in and obedi-

Muslim children embrace when greeting each other during the annual festival known as Eid al-Adha, or the Feast of Sacrifice.

ence to God under any and all circumstances. Thus, they see the hajj that Abraham created as a crucial renewal of faith. To celebrate that renewal, during Eid al-Adha each Muslim family that can afford to do so stages a large feast and invites several poor people to take part.

A second key holy feast day in Islam is Eid al-Fitr, or Feast of Fast Breaking, which occurs on the first day of the tenth Islamic month—Shawwal. The term *fast breaking* refers to the fact that on this day, directly following the close of Ramadan, Muslims break their monthlong dawn-to-dusk fast. During Eid al-Fitr, people not only hold banquets but also wear new clothes if they can afford them. In addition, they decorate their homes with colored lights and exchange gifts.

The Islamic prohibition against eating pork comes partly from the following verse in the Quran: "Forbidden to you for food are: dead meat, blood, the flesh of swine." The word *swine* generally refers to pigs. Muslims are not the only people who have a traditional objection to eating pork. Another is Jews, whose prohibition on eating pork is based on several biblical passages. One, from the book of Leviticus, reads: "And the swine, though he divide the hoof, and be cloven footed, yet he chews not the cud; he is unclean to you." Both Muslims and Jews cite essentially the same reasons for abstaining from eating pork. First, they argue that pigs have historically been known as scavengers that tend to live in very unclean conditions and are regularly covered in dirt and animal feces. In this view, the chances of humans consuming particles of such filth are high. Also, those who support the pork prohibition say medical research indicates that pork flesh sometimes contains various parasites. Among them are small but dangerous worms, including pinworm, roundworm, and hookworm. Particularly troublesome is the pork tapeworm, which, once ingested, takes up residence in the intestines. A tapeworm can grow to be extremely long, and its eggs can enter the bloodstream and from there travel to other parts of the body. If any of these eggs reach the brain, they can cause memory loss; if they make it into the heart, the result can be a heart attack.

Quran 5:3.

Leviticus 11:7.

Other Major Islamic Holidays

Ramadan itself is viewed by most Muslims as the most sacred of the Islamic holidays. It takes place during the ninth lunar month—called Ramadan in the festival's honor. The historical-spiritual basis of the holiday is that it was the month in which the angel Gabriel began helping Muhammad recite the verses of the Quran. To celebrate that momentous event, Muslims devote the month's entire twenty-nine days to alternately refraining from and then hugely enjoying the foods they see as part of God's bounty to humans. The belief is that this repeated daily fasting pleases

God because it continually brings his faithful followers together. As Carole Hillenbrand puts it, "The alternation of fasting in the day and shared meals taken with family and friends after nightfall strongly enhances Muslims' sense of community and social solidarity."[44]

Another Islamic holiday that commemorates an event directly related to Muhammad is Mawlid al-Nabi, the celebration of the Prophet's birthday. The feasting in his honor takes place on the twelfth day of the third lunar month—Rabi al-Awwal. In addition to the traditional banquet, people either recite or listen to someone else recite a religious sermon. There is also gift giving among relatives and friends.

Although a majority of Muslim sects observe Mawlid al-Nabi, a few do not. "The celebration is opposed by purists," Paul Grieve explains, "as magnifying the cult of Muhammad." Grieve says they feel this is "contrary to the true basis of Islam in which there are no intermediaries between man and God, with Muhammad regarded as nothing more than human. The feast is more popular in sentimental Pakistan, for example, than in the austere atmosphere of Saudi Arabia, where Mawlid is actively opposed."[45]

> *"[The] shared meals taken with family and friends after nightfall [during Ramadan] strongly enhances Muslims' sense of community."[44]*
>
> —Scholar Carole Hillenbrand

Still another popular Islamic holy day—Ashura—is observed differently by Sunnis and Shias. For Sunnis, the feast, held on the tenth day of the lunar month Muharram, recalls with respect and joy the time when God rescued a fellow People of the Book, the Jews, from their bondage in Egypt. Muhammad himself made this a compulsory Muslim holiday.

In contrast, although Shias also celebrate Ashura, they view its origins differently. The Shias' observance is a commemoration of the death of Muhammad's grandson, Husayn ibn Ali, in about 680 CE (or AH 58). The site of this event—Karbala, in central Iraq—thereafter became a place that Shia Muslims visit on a pilgrimage similar in some ways to the hajj. At the height of the Karbala

Shia men participate in a ritual procession as part of their observance of the Muslim holiday known as Ashura. Shia Muslims celebrate Ashura by commemorating the death in about 680 CE of Muhammad's grandson, Husayn ibn Ali.

festivities, a majestic passion play features actors who portray the stirring yet disturbing events surrounding Husayn's demise. (Because Husayn refused to pledge allegiance to the reigning caliph, Yazid, whom he viewed as illegitimate, Yazid had Husayn killed.)

Prohibited Activities and Behaviors

In addition to the regulations and expectations connected to annual holy days, Islam features bans on several social acts and behaviors. Some of the prohibited acts are viewed by nearly all Muslims as, variously, serious social breaches, crimes, or sins against God. Among them are worshipping false idols, engaging in sorcery, committing perjury, stealing from orphans or other helpless individuals, and disrespecting one's parents.

Seen as less extreme than those societal transgressions are a series of bans of more personal activities that most Muslims believe God wants people to avoid. Most, like drinking alcohol, are commonly practiced in non-Islamic cultures, particularly in Western democracies that have laws protecting personal freedom of expression. In Muslim cultures, in contrast, most people feel that God's will trumps personal freedom. In this view, God created these prohibitions, and even when people do not understand his reasons for doing so, he should be obeyed.

Most often those divine restrictions appear somewhere in the Quran. In the case of alcohol, it explains that at first it was allowed in the form of wine made from grapes and dates: "[It is from] the fruits of the date-palm, and grapes, whence you derive strong drink and also good nourishment."[46] Later, however, it became clear that some of the faithful were praying while drunk. In response, another Quranic verse warned against such acts: "O you who believe! Do not approach the prayer while you are drunk, so that you know what you say [to God]."[47] Finally, in a third Quranic verse, wine and other alcoholic drinks were banned entirely, as the Quran suggested that Satan used them to corrupt humans.

The Quran states in multiple sections that gambling is also to be avoided by Muslims. Usually, gambling is condemned in the same sections that prohibit the worship of idols (statues of gods) and divination (trying to foretell the future by examining natural signs). Verse 5:90, for example, states that all those activities derive from Satan and should be strictly avoided. To emphasize the point, the Quran's next section says, "Satan wants to provoke strife and hatred among you," through gambling and other unsavory acts "to prevent you from the remembrance of God, and from prayer. Will you not desist?"[48]

Eating pork falls into this same category of prohibitions, as does engaging in homosexual relations and practicing usury.

"Satan wants to provoke strife and hatred among you [in order] to prevent you from the remembrance of God."[48]

—The Quran

51

Muslim scholars define the latter as making money in unethical, unfair ways. One Quranic verse states, "God has made buying and selling lawful and usury unlawful."[49] There is nothing in the Quran or other major Islamic texts that condemns making a profit in business. Instead, it is making money solely by lending money—as in charging someone interest on a loan—that is seen as unethical. According to Tariq Ramadan, the ban is "based upon an economic philosophy that recognizes the right to profit from commerce all the while emphasizing that economic activity must serve humankind. Furthermore, money can only be produced by actual labor or by an exchange whose terms must be just, equitable, and transparent. Such a philosophy is fundamentally opposed to the [capitalist economic system]."[50]

Discouraged but Not Forbidden

Some other activities that have in modern times become common in social situations are not prohibited in the Quran. The most familiar examples are tobacco use, especially smoking, and the recreational use of various drugs. These were unknown substances in the cultures of Islam's early centuries, so no clear-cut rules regarding them developed.

In the past century or so, however, a number of Muslim legal scholars have recorded their opinions about tobacco and drug use. Some of these experts have tried to equate using them with drinking alcohol by reasoning through analogy, a process called *qiyas* in Arabic. That is, they argue that recreational drugs can produce more or less the same effects as alcohol. Among those effects can be reduced awareness of one's surroundings, negative impact on health, and/or addiction. Tobacco is also addictive and bad for human health, these experts point out. Therefore, by analogy, such substances should be avoided, just as alcohol is.

There is no way, however, that legal scholars can enforce their opinions on the entire Islamic community. The result is mixed reactions to the warnings given by those experts. Some Muslims follow their advice and refrain from using tobacco and recreational drugs. But many others ignore those well-meaning discouragements. Smoking is very common in some Muslim

The World Bank and other international organizations have studied the problem of the khat (or qat) addiction that is widespread in Yemen and to a lesser degree plagues some neighboring nations. Mustapha Rouis, a consultant for the World Bank, here explains some of the grave consequences of khat chewing.

> Qat use is linked to child malnutrition and food insecurity since household spending on it takes priority over spending on basic foodstuffs and essential medicines. The adverse health effects of qat include high blood-pressure, under-weight children (when pregnant women chew qat), cancer (from consuming pesticide residues on the qat leaves), and dental disease. Consumers spend an average of nearly 10 percent of their income on it, and the physical act of chewing the drug requires several hours a day. The culture of passing time chewing qat for much of the afternoon is inimical [contrary] to the development of a productive work force, with as much as one-quarter of usable working hours allocated to qat chewing. . . .
>
> The enormous amount of time spent chewing qat is time that in most other countries is typically spent in productive activities. Some 36 percent of users spend 2–4 hours per day chewing, 35 percent spend 4–6 hours a day, and an astonishing 22 percent spend more than 6 hours a day chewing qat. Most users believe that qat enhances their immediate work performance, but about a third report that the day after chewing qat, their work performance is impaired.

Mustapha Rouis, "Yemen's Qat Addiction Worsens," *Voices and Views: Middle East and North Africa* (blog), World Bank, March 20, 2014. http://blogs.worldbank.org.

countries, and in a few others the use of narcotics and other drugs for nonmedicinal purposes is deeply embedded in society.

An example of the latter is Yemen, which lies directly south of Saudi Arabia. There much of the population is addicted to the leaves of a plant called khat, or qat, which produces effects similar to those of cocaine. An estimated 90 percent of male

A farmer in Yemen prepares khat, a plant whose leaves, when chewed, release a substance that produces effects similar to those of cocaine. Although many Muslims refrain from smoking or using recreational drugs, the use of tobacco and even narcotics is common in some Muslim countries.

Yemenis and 25 percent of female ones chew the leaves on a regular basis. As the chewer holds a wad of leaves in the mouth, says a *Time* magazine investigator, "the khat slowly breaks down into the saliva and enters the bloodstream. The newcomer to Yemen's ancient capital can't miss the spectacle of almost an entire adult population presenting cheeks bulging with cud, leaving behind green confetti of discarded leaves and branches. For its many devotees, khat is a social lubricant on a par with coffee or alcohol in the West."[51]

Although large numbers of Yemenis who use khat agree that chewing it is a bad habit, they also "do not feel that they can stop using qat on their own," World Bank consultant Mustapha Rouis reports. In surveys of thousands of khat users taken by the World Bank in 2015 and 2016, he writes, a majority of the respondents "declared that government intervention is necessary to address the qat problem."[52]

It is possible that government action may indeed be necessary, at least in the short term, to curb khat's use. This is largely because no firm or universal Islamic religious rules against it have yet been formulated. Some Islamic legal experts have spoken out against it. For example, Saudi scholar Muhammad ibn Ibrahim recommended that khat be banned because "it leads to harms that affect a Muslim's mind, religion, and body and wastes their money leaving them severely addicted to many evils."[53] Ibn Ibrahim's opinion lacks the weight of the Quran and other core Islamic texts, however. At present, those sacred writings remain the principal sources, justifications, and enforcers of the faith's main rules of conduct.

CHAPTER FIVE

What Challenges Does Islam Face in the Modern World?

Like other major world religions, Islam has faced and continues to face a number of challenges, some from within and others from outside its own ranks. One of the largest of these challenges is the ongoing pressure of modernity—including rapidly advancing technology and an increasingly interconnected global society. More and more, political ideas and popular culture from Western nations steadily seep into and affect traditional Muslim cultures. The latter tend to be inward looking, politically conservative, and less socially permissive than most Western cultures. So Muslim countries often find themselves struggling to maintain long-accepted traditions while keeping up with the modern world.

A good example is the changing treatment of women in Saudi Arabia. There women long lacked the civil rights and social freedom that Saudi men enjoyed. But as women in other parts of the world demanded, and in many cases gained, equal rights with men, it became clear to some Saudi leaders that they could no longer continue to lag behind the rest of the world. In 2018 Saudi women were finally allowed to drive cars and attend soccer matches in public stadiums, and the lifting of other restrictions on women is in the works.

Although the efforts to keep pace with fast-changing modern life can be daunting for the global Islamic community, that challenge in many ways pales before another that has descended on that community in the past few decades. Namely, Islam and its followers have acquired a decidedly negative image in other parts of the world, particularly in Western nations such as the United States and Britain.

That image, Reza Aslan explains, is one of a religion whose members are inherently prone to violence. Many in the West, he says, have come to view Islam as a "warrior religion." Tarnished by that depiction, most or even all Muslims are frequently assumed to be, or at least to sympathize with, Islamist terrorists. The stereotypical image that many peace-loving Muslims have been branded with, Aslan continues, is of a person "strapped with explosives, ready to be martyred for God, eager to take as many innocent people as possible with him."[54]

A Muslim woman proudly takes the wheel of a car in Jidda, Saudi Arabia. Gaining permission to drive is one of a number of ways in which Saudi women are beginning to gain the rights and freedoms that men have long enjoyed.

The al Qaeda Attacks

That image of Islam as a violent warrior religion, which most Muslims reject as untrue and unfair, is not new, Aslan and other scholars point out. Indeed, as far back as the medieval era, Western societies periodically depicted Muslims as sword-wielding fanatics bent on conquest. Moreover, it was common well into the twentieth century for Western history texts to claim that those conquerors forced the defeated peoples to convert to Islam. The reality is that this charge is false, says modern scholar of Middle Eastern cultures Bernard Lewis. It is true that medieval Muslim armies conquered other peoples, he writes. But so did European armies, right up into modern times. Furthermore, Lewis explains, the non-Muslim subjects of the lands that Muslims defeated "enjoyed the free exercise of their religion, normal property rights, and were very frequently employed in the service of the state."[55]

That old stereotype of sword-waving Muslim warriors was replaced with another one—that of bomb-wielding Islamist terrorists—beginning in the late twentieth century. This was largely the result of the attacks perpetrated around the globe by terrorist groups like al Qaeda and ISIS. Spearheading these assaults at first were al Qaeda's leaders, Osama bin Laden and Ayman al-Zawahiri.

"[Muslims should] kill Americans and their allies, civilians, and military."[56]

—Al Qaeda leaders Osama bin Laden and Ayman al-Zawahiri

In February 1998 these two men issued what they claimed was an Islamic legal decree certified by religious authorities. Whether that was true remains unknown. The fact is that neither Bin Laden nor al-Zawahiri was a religious authority, and most Islamic religious leaders would surely have rejected the decree.

That public statement said in part: "To kill Americans and their allies, civilians, and military is an individual duty of every Muslim who is able, in any country where this is possible." The decree went on, "We call on every Muslim who believes in God and hopes for reward to obey God's command to kill the Americans and plunder their possessions wherever he finds them and whenever he can."[56]

In this excerpt from one of his popular books about Islam, noted scholar of religions Reza Aslan provides a thumbnail sketch of where he believes the image of Islam as a faith practiced by marauding soldiers originated.

> [The] deep-rooted stereotype of Islam as a warrior religion has its origins in the papal propaganda of the Crusades, where Muslims were depicted as the soldiers of the Anti-Christ in blasphemous occupation of the Holy Lands (and far more importantly, of the silk route to China). In the Middle Ages, while Muslim philosophers, scientists, and mathematicians were preserving the knowledge of the past and determining the scholarship of the future, a belligerent and deeply fractured Holy Roman Empire tried to distinguish itself from the Turks who were strangling it from all sides by labeling Islam "the religion of the sword," as though there were in that era an alternative means of territorial expansion besides war. And as the European colonialists of the eighteenth and nineteenth centuries systematically plundered the natural resources of the Middle East and North Africa . . . the image of the dreaded Muslim warrior, clad in a long robe and brandishing his scimitar [curved sword] became a widely popular literary cliché. It still is.

Reza Aslan, *No God but God: The Origins, Evolution, and Future of Islam*. New York: Random House, 2011, p. 80.

Only a few months later, in August 1998, al Qaeda bombed the US embassies in the African countries of Tanzania and Kenya, killing some 220 people. Bin Laden's operatives also blew a hole in an American ship, the USS *Cole*, while it was anchored off Yemen's coast. Finally, al Qaeda launched the infamous 9/11 attacks, which on September 11, 2001, destroyed the World Trade Center towers in New York City, killing close to three thousand people.

A Badly Stained Image of Islam

These attacks by Islamist terrorists generated two main responses in the United States and other Western countries. The first was to label the attackers heinous criminals and make a concerted effort to find and punish them. The other response was more emotional. Large numbers of Americans and other Westerners jumped to the conclusion that most or all Muslims supported or approved of the attacks, reasoning that the Islamic faith is violent at its core.

Some Americans who felt that way pointed to the fact that a few members of al Qaeda had publicly cited passages from the Quran that they claimed justified their violent actions. One of those passages states, "Fight against them [the nonbelievers] so that Allah will punish them by your hands and disgrace them and give you victory over them and heal the breasts of a believing people."[57] Also frequently cited was a Quranic excerpt that says: "Those who believe [in Allah] follow the Truth from their Lord. Thus does Allah set forth their descriptions for men. So when you meet in battle those who disbelieve, smite the necks."[58]

Thus, the 9/11 attacks, along with other later violent acts by al Qaeda and other Islamist terrorists, convinced many Americans that Islam encourages violence. In the summer of 2003, the widely respected Pew Research Center conducted a poll that found that 44 percent of Americans—well over 100 million people—believed Islam was more likely to foster violence than other religions. Moreover, non-Muslim dislike and harassment of Muslims in the United States sharply increased. In the year before 9/11, the Pew Research Center reported, there had been only twelve violent assaults on Muslims in the country. That number rose to an alarming ninety-three in the year following the 9/11 attacks.

The badly stained image of Islam that developed after al Qaeda's attacks on the West persists more or less unchanged today, although this attitude is based only partly on al Qaeda's actions. The beheadings, rapes, and other crimes of ISIS, as well as the violence of another Islamist terror group, the Taliban in Afghanistan, have generated numerous headlines in the years since 9/11. A 2017 Pew Research Center survey showed the same proportion of Americans as before—44 percent—have an unfavorable view of Islam. Many of the respondents also said there seemed to be a natural conflict between Islam and Western-style democracy.

Most Muslims Reject Terrorism

That notion about Muslims—that as a group they are far more prone to violence and unethical deeds than non-Muslims—is be-

Arab men and women do their shopping in a traditional market in Lebanon. Most Muslims thoroughly disapprove of the terrorism perpetrated by Islamist extremists.

lied by the fact that most Muslims thoroughly disapprove of the Islamist extremists. Several Pew and other surveys taken between 2014 and 2017 found that the vast majority of the residents of several Muslim nations and communities deplore al Qaeda and ISIS. Close to 100 percent of those interviewed in Lebanon, for example, felt that way; so did 94 percent of Jordan's residents. Also, most Muslims questioned for the surveys said that suicide bombings and other kinds of violence against civilians in the name of Islam are unjustified. In Indonesia, the world's most populous Muslim nation, 92 percent of respondents said that, and 91 percent of Iraqi Muslims answered the same.

Tariq Ramadan, himself a devout Muslim, points out that more moderate modern Muslims have sometimes committed violent

An organization called the Muslim Public Affairs Council (MPAC) seeks to improve the image of Islam and Muslims in general by encouraging the elimination of stereotypes of Muslims and their religion in movies and TV shows. In late 2017 representatives of the MPAC met with members of the film industry and discussed how moviemakers might keep from perpetuating Muslim typecasting. Also, in a public event attended by members of the Writers Guild Foundation and MPAC's Hollywood division, several suggestions were offered for how to bring about more authentic film portrayals of Islam and Muslims. The MPAC's Hollywood division, run by Sue Obeidi, regularly works with production companies in an effort to create such accurate portrayals. In 2018 Obeidi and her associates worked closely with the makers of Disney's live-action version of *Aladdin*, ABC's *Grey's Anatomy*, Hulu's *The Looming Tower*, NatGeo's *The State*, Paramount/Amazon's *Tom Clancy's Jack Ryan*, and Nickelodeon's *Glitch Techs*. Obeidi says:

> I want to make sure that to us [MPAC] ultimate success is not having a Muslim TV network, but to have Muslims at the helm of a major network, studio, and production company. In order to really make a difference in the narrative, we cannot afford to be burning daylight by preaching to the choir. Muslims, like all other members of vulnerable communities, need to be in decision-making roles at major mainstream TV networks, studios, and production companies.

Obeidi adds that she is hopeful there will be a Muslim lead on a television drama and sitcom sometime in the next few years.

Quoted in Courtney Idasetima, "Industry Panel Suggests Ways to Better Represent Muslims in Film and TV," *Hollywood Reporter*, December 11, 2017. www.hollywoodreporter.com.

acts. But more often than not, he claims, such armed force was justified and should not be equated with the terrorism of al Qaeda and ISIS. "Though we abhor violence," he writes, "we cannot place armed resistance to oppression and struggles for national liberation on the same footing as terrorism. No serious, self-respecting historian or political analyst would tolerate such confusion of terms, and yet we frequently find a total lack of nuance and caution in analysis produced in the West." Regardless of why Muslims or other people resort to violence, Ramadan adds, "as a matter of principle, it is imperative at all times to condemn the murder of civilians and innocents." Their deaths, he says, "are never justifiable."[59]

Hate Crimes and Discrimination on the Rise

The fact that Islam's image has been tainted a great deal by the acts of the most extreme Muslims has led to distrust of Muslims in the United States and some other Western nations. In 2017 the Pew Research Center found that there are about 3.5 million Muslims of all ages in the United States, making up about 1.1 percent of Americans overall. That entire segment of the population has come under suspicion by a large and at times quite vocal minority of non-Muslim Americans. The Pew Research Center found that in 2016 fully 49 percent of Americans thought that at least some Muslim citizens were anti-American.

One result of these bad feelings was that hate crimes perpetrated by non-Muslims against Muslims have increased in number in recent years in the United States. (A hate crime is defined in *Newsweek* as "a criminal offense motivated by either race, ethnicity, religion, disability, sexual orientation, gender or gender identity."[60]) According to a recent survey, the number of assaults against Muslims in the United States rose significantly between 2015 and 2016. In the latter year alone, at least 127 American Muslims suffered physical assaults—36 percent more than in 2001, the year of the 9/11 attacks.

What is more, overall incidences of discrimination against American Muslims are on the rise. Pew researcher Katayoun Kishi reports that in 2017, "half of U.S. Muslim adults [said] that in recent years it has become more difficult to be a Muslim in the U.S., with 10% of this group attributing this to discrimination, racism, and prejudice. In general, nearly a quarter of U.S. Muslim adults

> *"It is imperative at all times to condemn the murder of civilians and innocents."[59]*
>
> —Oxford University scholar Tariq Ramadan

viewed discrimination, racism, or prejudice as the most important problem facing American Muslims today."[61]

One of the more publicized examples of this anti-Muslim prejudice occurred in May 2017 in Portland, Oregon. Two young Muslim women who were minding their own business on a local train came under vicious verbal attack by a non-Muslim white

Agents from the Bureau of Alcohol, Tobacco, Firearms, and Explosives (ATF) and other government agencies search for clues in the rubble of a burned mosque in Victoria, Texas. Hate crimes against Muslims have been on the rise in the United States in recent years.

man. When three other non-Muslim men intervened to stop him, he stabbed two of them to death and wounded the third. "It's horrific," commented Sergeant Pete Simpson, a spokesperson for the Portland Police Bureau, shortly after the killer was arrested. "There are no other words to describe what happened today."[62] In another incident that same year, a white man whom local police called an anti-Muslim bigot burned down a mosque in Victoria, Texas.

Attempts to Reshape Islam's Image

The challenge of improving Islam's image in the West and around the world is no less than immense, say political, religious, and other experts both inside and outside the global Muslim community. Reshaping that image in a positive way is vital, says Egyptian social and political commentator Hussein Amin. "This is important for both the East and the West," he points out. "For us, not achieving this will be disastrous, because our contacts with the outside world will weaken. The economic effects will be disastrous. [Meanwhile] on the part of the West, to feel hatred toward a whole people and culture can't lead to a comfortable situation. They will lose the real contribution that Islam can make to world civilization."[63]

Some Western countries are actively making an effort to help Muslims project a fairer, more positive image. One is Britain, where polls indicate that a majority of the non-Muslim population associates Islam with religious extremism. Since 2010 a London-based organization—the Exploring Islam Foundation—has diligently been trying to refurbish that faith's image among average Britons.

The group's main approach is to launch various media campaigns. The most familiar and well received consists of advertisements posted in subway stations, taxicabs, buses, and so

> *"Nearly a quarter of U.S. Muslim adults [view] discrimination . . . as the most important problem facing American Muslims today."*[61]
>
> —Researcher Katayoun Kishi of the Pew Research Center

forth. One shows a woman wearing a traditional Muslim head scarf, with the caption "I believe in rights for women. So did Muhammad." Another poster displays German-born former MTV host Kristiane Backer and bears the words "I believe in protecting the environment. So did Muhammad." The Exploring Islam Foundation's campaigns director, Remona Aly, told an interviewer, "Our goal now is to put forth the universal values that Muslims hold, which are ones of justice, of compassion, of mutual understanding and tolerance."[64]

Be More Active and Visible?

Similar efforts to improve Islam's image are ongoing in the United States. One of the organizations working toward that goal is the nonprofit Muslim Public Affairs Council (MPAC), based in Washington, DC, and Los Angeles. A spokesperson for the group admits that the task of showing Islam's good side is difficult in America, where the public has encountered few positive images of Muslims:

> The sad part is that what little information Americans do get about Islam centers on such negative and horrid events such as bombings, beheadings, and terror. It is only reasonable to expect a negative reaction. If one is inundated with images of people who claim to be Muslims acting as barbarians who have no place in a civilized world, what can we expect? The problem is that the general American population has little in terms of positive counter-images.
>
> If we American Muslims want to improve public perception of ourselves, we must be more present, more active, and more visible.[65]

Following that reasoning, the MPAC seeks to urge and help American Muslims to become engaged not only in their local Islamic communities but also in the larger American cultural melting pot. On a community level, the MPAC teaches Muslims to become activists armed with knowledge about the US government system, American popular culture, and the many religions that flourish in the United States. The hope is that these individuals will go out into their communities and use that knowledge in friendly discussions with non-Muslims. In addition, the organization urges Muslims to talk about positive Islamic values in newspaper and television interviews, as well as to run for public office if they are so inclined.

In general, the MPAC spokesperson says, "on an individual level, we need to be social with co-workers; run for local office; be a part of the PTA; join a softball league; or volunteer at a soup kitchen." All of these activities, along with others like them, will help, because after all, it is only natural for people to "fear what they do not understand." Therefore, "let's help them understand!"[66]

> *"To improve public perception of ourselves, we must be more present, more active, and more visible."*[65]
>
> —The Muslim Public Affairs Council

SOURCE NOTES

Introduction: The Remarkable Unity of Islam

1. Quoted in Religious Tolerance, "A Muslim Prayer for Peace and Religious Tolerance." www.religioustolerance.org.
2. Quoted in Ali Mamouri, "Who Are the Kharijites and What Do They Have to Do with ISIS?," Al-Monitor, 2015. www.al-monitor.com.
3. Tariq Ramadan, *Introduction to Islam*. New York: Oxford University Press, 2017, p. 99.
4. Ramadan, *Introduction to Islam*, p. 77.
5. Ramadan, *Introduction to Islam*, p. 112.
6. Ramadan, *Introduction to Islam*, p. 115.

Chapter One: The Origins of Islam

7. Reza Aslan, *No God but God: The Origins, Evolution, and Future of Islam*. New York: Random House, 2011, p. 6.
8. Aslan, *No God but God*, p. 7.
9. Paul Grieve, *Islam: History, Faith and Politics: The Complete Introduction*. New York: Carroll and Graf, 2006, p. 44.
10. Grieve, *Islam*, p. 44.
11. Aslan, *No God but God*, p. 34.
12. Quran 96:1–5.
13. Grieve, *Islam*, p. 48.
14. Carole Hillenbrand, *Introduction to Islam*. New York: Thames and Hudson, 2015, p. 33.
15. Quoted in Aslan, *No God but God*, p. 111.

Chapter Two: What Do Muslims Believe?

16. Quran 20:4–8.
17. Quran 2:255.
18. Grieve, *Islam*, p. 88.
19. Quran 38:71–78.
20. Quran 47:32–34.
21. Quran 22:19–22.
22. Quran 9:72.

23. Quran 13:23–24.
24. Hillenbrand, *Introduction to Islam*, p. 68.
25. Quran 3:46.
26. Quran 3:49–51.
27. Grieve, *Islam*, p. 274.

Chapter Three: How Do Muslims Practice Their Faith?

28. Aslan, *No God but God*, p. 147.
29. Ramadan, *Introduction to Islam*, p. 74.
30. Quoted in New Muslim Guide, "Testimony of Faith: Meaning and Requirements." http://newmuslimguide.com.
31. Ramadan, *Introduction to Islam*, p. 75.
32. Hillenbrand, *Introduction to Islam*, p. 92.
33. Quran 107:4–6.
34. Grieve, *Islam*, p. 109.
35. Quoted in Huda, "The Adhan: The Islamic Call to Prayer," ThoughtCo, June 28, 2017. www.thoughtco.com.
36. Quran 2:215.
37. Grieve, *Islam*, p. 112.
38. Neal Robinson, *Islam: A Concise Introduction*. Washington, DC: Georgetown University Press, 1999, p. 148.
39. BBC, "Hajj: Pilgrimage to Mecca," August 9, 2009. www.bbc .co.uk.
40. Aslan, *No God but God*, p. 28.
41. Quran 5:8.
42. Hillenbrand, *Introduction to Islam*, p. 242.

Chapter Four: Rules to Live By

43. Quran 2:127.
44. Hillenbrand, *Introduction to Islam*, p. 103.
45. Grieve, *Islam*, p. 212.
46. Quran 16:67.
47. Quran 4:43.
48. Quran 5:91.
49. Quran 2:275.
50. Ramadan, *Introduction to Islam*, p. 93.
51. Andrew L. Butters, "Is Yemen Chewing Itself to Death?," *Time*, August 25, 2009. http://content.time.com.

52. Mustapha Rouis, "Yemen's Qat Addiction Worsens," *Voices and Views: Middle East and North Africa* (blog), World Bank, March 20, 2014. http://blogs.worldbank.org.
53. Quoted in Mohamad Abdalla and Abdi Hersi, "Khat: Islamic Legal Perspective," Australian Institute of Criminology, 2011. www.aic.gov.au.

Chapter Five: What Challenges Does Islam Face in the Modern World?

54. Aslan, *No God but God*, p. 80.
55. Bernard Lewis, *The Arabs in History*. New York: Oxford University Press, 2002, p. 94.
56. Osama bin Laden, "Osama bin Laden's 1998 Fatwa," Federation of American Scientists. www.911memorial.org.
57. Quran 9:14.
58. Quran 47:3.
59. Ramadan, *Introduction to Islam*, p. 195.
60. Quoted in Brian Levin, "Islamophobia in America: Rise in Hate Crimes Against Muslims Shows What Politicians Say Matters," *Newsweek*, July 21, 2017. www.newsweek.com.
61. Katayoun Kishi, "Assaults Against Muslims in U.S. Surpass 2001 Levels," Pew Research Center, November 15, 2017. www.pewresearch.org.
62. Quoted in Matthew Haag and Jacey Fortin, "Two Killed in Portland While Trying to Stop Anti-Muslim Rant, Police Say," *New York Times*, May 27, 2017. www.nytimes.com.
63. Quoted in Sarah Gauch, "How to Correct Islam's Bad Image in the West," *Christian Science Monitor*, November 26, 2001. www.csmonitor.com.
64. Quoted in Olly Barrat, "Poster Campaign Aims to Improve Image of Islam in the UK," Deutsche Welle, 2018. www.dw.com.
65. Muslim Public Affairs Council, "Fear of the Unknown: How to Improve Perceptions of Muslims," April 22, 2015. www.mpac.org.
66. Muslim Public Affairs Council, "Fear of the Unknown."

FOR FURTHER RESEARCH

Books

Mihahel Ashkan, *Islam*. Broomall, PA: Mason Crest, 2017.

Steven Crane, *Basics of Islam: A Christian's Guide to Understanding Islam*. Star, ID: Endurance, 2017.

Bridey Heing, *Cultural Destruction by ISIS*. Berkeley Heights, NJ: Enslow, 2018.

Gabriel Iqbal, *Illustrated Encyclopedia of the Golden Age of Islam*. Oakville, ON: Eureka Academy, 2015.

Eugene Rogan, *The Arabs: A History*. New York: Basic Books, 2017.

Ziauddin Sardar, *Prophet Muhammad: A Short Biography*. Markfield, UK: Kube, 2018.

Internet Sources

BBC, "Muslim Holy Days," July 9, 2009. www.bbc.co.uk/religion/religions/islam/holydays/holydays.shtml.

Biography, "Muhammad," 2018. www.biography.com/people/muhammad.

CNN, "Islam: Fast Facts," September 21, 2017. www.cnn.com/2013/11/12/world/islam-fast-facts.

Michael Lipka and Conrad Hackett, "Why Muslims Are the World's Fastest-Growing Religious Group," Pew Research Center, April 6, 2017. www.pewresearch.org/fact-tank/2017/04/06/why-muslims-are-the-worlds-fastest-growing-religious-group.

Spahic Omer, "Islam and Modernity," IslamiCity, March 28, 2016. www.islamicity.org/9110/islam-and-modernity.

Pew Research Center, "U.S. Muslims Concerned About Their Place in Society, but Continue to Believe in the American Dream," July 26, 2017. www.pewforum.org/2017/07/26/findings-from-pew-research-centers-2017-survey-of-us-muslims.

Websites

A Brief Illustrated Guide to Understanding Islam (www.islam -guide.com). One of the most detailed and accurate sites about Islam, this one is based on a book on the same topic. It has numerous links to articles, fact boxes, biographies of important figures, and much more.

Islam: The Second Largest World Religion, Religious Tolerance (www.religioustolerance.org/islam.htm). This extensive website contains many dozens of links leading to factual information on nearly all aspects of Islamic belief, rules, and practices.

Quran (www.clearquran.com). Easy and convenient to use, this site features a simple translation of the Quran that can be used for reference or study. By clicking on the drop-down menu beside the word *Quran* at the top, visitors can choose from the 114 sections and go directly to the desired one.

INDEX

74

PICTURE CREDITS

ABOUT THE AUTHOR

Historian and award-winning author Don Nardo has written numerous books about the ancient and medieval worlds, their peoples, and their cultures, including the birth and growth of the major religions in those societies. Nardo, who also composes and arranges orchestral music, lives with his wife, Christine, in Massachusetts.